This Book
longs

E L E M E N T A R Y
TAROT

Roberta Peters

Published in the United Kingdom in 2000 by Caxton Editions
20 Bloomsbury Street
London WC1B 3QA
a member of the Caxton Publishing Group

© Copyright 2000 Caxton Publishing Group

Designed and Produced for Caxton Editions by Open Door Limited
80 High Street, Colsterworth, Lincolnshire, NG33 5JA
Illustration: Andrew Shepherd, Art Angle
Colour separation: GA Graphics Stamford

Title: Elementary TAROT
ISBN: 1-84067-244-7

Picture credits
Images Colour Library: 7, 12, 13, 14, 15, 75

ELEMENTARY
TAROT

Roberta Peters

CAXTON EDITIONS

CONTENTS

CONTENTS

INTRODUCTION

When I started out as a Tarot reader over a quarter of a century ago, the picture was very different from today, because Tarot cards were then considered to be "occult" and frightening. Clients who were happy to have their hands read or to have an astrological chart erected and interpreted were nervous of the Tarot. Some were convinced that if they were to have a reading, something nasty would be called up from beyond to disturb their peaceful nights. Nowadays, Tarot reading is the kind of popular pastime that tea-leaf reading or playing card reading once was, and professional Tarot readers advertise in magazines, give readings on the air and even on-line. Books and software proliferate, and while Tarot has gained in popularity it has lost its unnerving occult image, and this comfortable familiarity makes it appear harmless. So has the Tarot lost its power? Not at·all. The cards are still a frighteningly accurate way of peering into life of a perfect stranger and of predicting his future.

When a media person asks me to give an explanation of why the cards work, I usually shrug my shoulders and leave it at that. It is easy to say that the archetypes on the cards resonate with our unconscious minds, but this begs the question of why certain cards emerge in order to tell their tale. My reasoning is that a person seeking a Tarot reading is himself guided by spiritual forces to seek out such a reading. For example, if the Questioner is given a warning about an impending problem, he must take it seriously, while reassurance about future decisions helps him to move ahead with confidence.

Right: An original card from the A. E. Waite Pack of 1910 designed by Pamela Colman-Smith in Collaboration with Arthur Edward Waite – Card 15 – The Devil.

TAROT MYTHS

There are many myths surrounding the Tarot, and one states that you should never buy your own Tarot cards. This makes no sense at all, because if you don't go choose a set of cards that suit you, how can you feel happy when using them? Once you have bought your Tarot deck you should regard it as an important tool and not allow others to handle it without your permission.

How you keep your cards is a matter of personal preference. Many readers buy or make a special purse for their cards and most like to wrap them in a silk scarf. I am a sucker for attractive boxes which I buy to keep my many sets of cards in. The idea of silk being spiritually protective is another myth. Good quality heavy silk is hard to cut or penetrate, so in days gone by, Japanese warriors wrapped their bodies in it so that if they were shot by an arrow it would enter the body, carrying the silk along with it. This meant that the arrow could safely be pulled out of the body and the chances of infection were greatly reduced. It has become a Tarot tradition to keep the cards wrapped in a piece of silk but there is no need to if you don't want to. I simply keep my cards loose in their box.

Another myth is that it is bad luck to read the cards for yourself, but it is perfectly natural for anybody to want to give themselves a reading and we all do it. The only caveat is that you won't end up with as good a reading as you would from a stranger, because you are too close to your own life and your own problems. Much the same goes when you try to give readings to loved-ones or close friends.

I once heard someone say that it is "bad form" to read the cards for a third party. For example, if a Questioner wants to know what is going on in the mind of her lover, but Tarot cards are designed to look into everything that is going on around the Questioner, including what is in the mind of his lover, colleague or friend.

EMOTION IS A PSYCHIC LOCOMOTIVE

A Tarot reading reaches for the most emotive event in the life of a Questioner. Therefore, if his health is fine but his domestic circumstances are a mess; that is what will show up in a reading. One difficulty that Tarot readers can face comes when dealing with a Questioner who has experienced a major upheaval in his past but whose present and future is uneventful. The way to deal with this is to mentally ask your spiritual guides to show you the future and either lay out another spread from the deck as it stands, or give the cards back to the Questioner for another quick shuffle, but without repeating the cutting and turning stage. The worst case that I ever experienced was when I gave a reading to a lady who was absolutely fascinated to find that the reading was perfect in every detail – except for the fact that the events that I described had happened forty years previously!

BEFORE GIVING A READING

Tarot books suggest that you find a quiet place with a nice table that is covered by an attractive cloth for your work. As a professional Tarot reader, I can tell you that it is quite normal to give a reading amid the chaos of a psychic festival, or on the tiny ledge allocated to a guest in a radio station. Professionals give readings over the phone, on the corner of someone's office table, on the floor, on a bed or in the open air. None of these places are ideal but it proves that you don't need a perfect venue. However, if you are new to the Tarot it is better to allow yourself to settle into a quiet, calm state of mind before you begin your reading. It is also worth mentally asking for spiritual guidance before you begin.

Ask your Questioner to shuffle the cards thoroughly and then cut them. Tradition says that he should use his left hand when cutting the cards and to cut them into three piles, moving towards the left. Then he should put the cards back into one pile in any order they choose and hand them back to you.

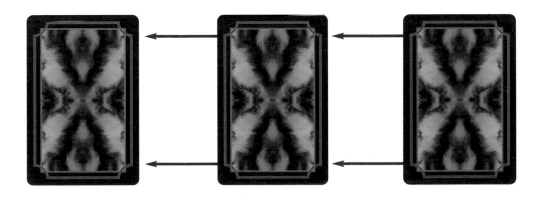

Most Tarot readers use the cards only in the upright position. If you choose to use the cards in both the upright and reversed positions the easiest thing is to ask your questioner to stir the cards around on the table rather than shuffling them, and then to put them back into one deck again. After your Questioner has shuffled or stirred the cards, take them back with the edge that was closest to him now facing you and then lay them out in a side to side manner so that they remain in the position that they occupied when in your Questioner's hands.

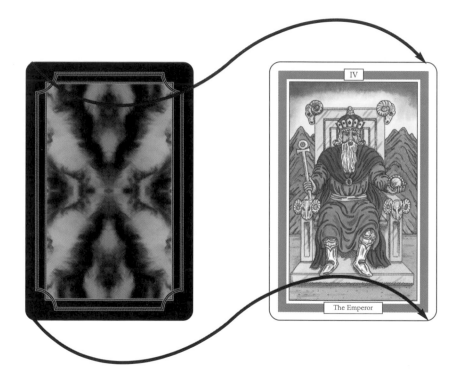

THE MAJOR AND MINOR ARCANA

The word "Arcana" comes from the word arcane, which means hidden, secret, known only by a select few and so on. The Major Arcana is a set of 22 separate cards, each of which holds a powerful image. The Minor Arcana cards are far more specific in nature, talking as they do about love, career, wealth, domestic life and so forth. There are four suits in the Minor Arcana and in this book and deck they are known as Wands, Cups, Pentacles and Swords. In other decks the Pentacles can be called Coins and the Wands can be called Rods, Staves and even Sticks.

THE COURT CARDS

Each suit of the Minor Arcana carries four Court cards, these being the King, Queen, Knight and Page. In some decks, the Knight and Page are called the Prince and Princess, but the Knight/Page combination is far more usual. In a reading, the King and Queen are seen as mature adults, the Knight usually represent a young man and the pages either young girls or children. How one describes a person from the cards is a matter of experience and also of individual preference. You can use systems that are based upon astrology, colouring, general appearance, the nature of a person or pure intuition – or a combination of any of the above. This sounds vague and unhelpful but sooner or later every Tarot reader finds something that works for him.

As you read through the text you will find zodiac signs that are associated with the suits and a general description of the nature of each court card personality. The good news is that using the Tarot will develop your intuitive and psychic gifts, so you will soon be able to "feel" the nature of the person on the cards. A court card can refer to the person for whom you are doing the reading.

THE HISTORY OF TAROT

Nobody knows for certain where the Tarot originated, some say it was ancient Egypt and others suggest 10th century China or Korea. What does appear certain is that fortune telling cards were carried and used by Gypsies as they moved both westward and south east through Europe and Asia, ahead of the invading Mongol and Turkish armies. It seems likely that the images depicted on the cards altered as they travelled along, abandoning archetypes that meant nothing to each set of new clients in each new country, in favour of those that they could understand. Early card images may have been absorbed from those that originated in any country in Asia and the Orient, also Greece, Egypt, Israel and the Celtic countries. Both chess and playing cards are a spin-off from the Tarot, and in all these cases the images are of medieval kings, queens and knights. This leads us to suppose that these early cards were not only adapted to make sense to those who used them, but also designed to flatter the Gypsies' early "clients".

It is possible that the original European Tarot was created in order to amuse and pacify a king who was fast descending into madness. In February 1392, Charles Poupart, the treasurer for King Charles VI of France made a payment entry in his books for three gilt decks that were painted for Charles by Jacquemin Gringonneur. Charles went mad in the same year. It is known that other illustrations found their way into decks of Tarot-like cards during the 14th and 15th centuries. The earliest Tarot deck of the type that modern Tarot readers could just about use is the Visconti-Sforza deck which was hand painted in the mid-fifteenth century. It is possible to track down copies of this beautiful deck even today. The Visconti-Sforza deck was created at the time of the marriage of Bianca Maria Visconti, daughter of the feared Filippo Maria Visconti, Duke of Milan, to the professional soldier, Francesco Sforza in 1441. The original deck contained 74 cards. It is interesting to note that some of the items pictured on these cards that have long been accepted as spiritual inspiration were actually heraldic emblems that belonged to the Visconti and Sforza families! Imagine such a deck being created for a powerful ruling elite in our own time. Would it depict the stars and stripes perhaps? And would this symbol eventually become translated into a truly "spiritual" image five centuries hence?

Above: the Knight of Swords designed by Scalpini in 1983 – a recreation of the Visconti pack.

Left: A reproduction of The Moon card of the Charles VI set of Tarot cards.

Far left:The Valet of Cups of a Tarot series designed in Bologna in 1664.

Left: The 16th Major Trump (The Falling Tower, or House of God) of the Tarot set in various designs. Top right is the traditional Marseilles design.

Below: Card 10, Wheel of Fortune. An original card from the 1910 edition of Tarot cards designed by Pamela Colman-Smith, in Collaboration with Arthur Edward Waite.

A 15th century sermon against the cards talks about the four suits and the Major Arcana as two separate types of card, so these may not have been amalgamated into one deck until later. It appears that some form of playing cards came to Italy via north Africa, but whether these were Tarot is not known. Most early Tarot decks were Italian, but French ones soon followed. One early deck that is still in use today is the Tarot de Marseilles which is based on woodblock prints. This has the familiar suits of Rods, Cups, Coins and Swords depicted upon the cards, in addition to the court cards of the Minor Arcana and the strange trump cards of the Major Arcana. During the 19th century, Eliphas Levi linked the cards to the Kabala and later A. E. Waite and Aleister Crowley linked them to astrology.

WHEEL of FORTUNE

THE MAJOR ARCANA

INTRODUCTION

The Major Arcana of the Tarot is very mysterious. It is not a suit as such, but a series of 22 separate cards, each with its own individual meaning.

The Major Arcana of the Tarot upset religious people in the past – and it still does, due to the apparently religious images that are on some of the cards. These days, Tarot card readers adapt the archetypes of the Major Arcana cards to suit modern life rather than concentrating the medieval ideas behind most of these cards. The Major Arcana cards are numbered from one to 21, except for the Fool which is numbered zero and which can be read as the first or the last of the Major Arcana group – or indeed both.

These cards are powerful but each one alone does not make up a reading and they need to be accompanied by other cards in order to make sense. It is usually the surrounding Minor Arcana cards that fill in the gaps. For instance, the Wheel of Fortune card simply means that a major change is on the way, and it is the surrounding cards that will show whether this is in the area of relationships, work, the home, health or any other facet of your life.

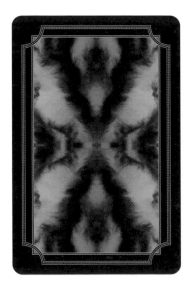

The Fool

The Magician

The High Priestess

The Empress

The Emperor

The Hierophant

The Lovers

The Chariot

Strength

The Hermit

The Wheel of Fortune

Justice

The Hanged Man

Death

Temperance

The Devil

The Tower

The Star

The Moon

The Sun

Judgement

The World

THE FOOL – 0
A beginning, a fresh start

0

The Fool

adventure. Whatever this card represented in years gone by, to modern Tarot readers the Fool signifies the beginning of an enterprise.

This is the moment of birth when you embark on something completely new, without prior knowledge or experience. You may be completely unprepared for what is to come but this card suggests that spiritual guidance and protection is at hand. The light-hearted feeling about this card denotes that the new enterprise will be quite entertaining.

The character in the illustration is close to the edge of a cliff: he appears happy, he has his friendly little dog along with him for company and he carries a bag containing his necessities on the end of his staff. The indications are that even if he falls from the cliff, he will be all right. He is young, innocent and clearly about to embark on an

REVERSED
There is a warning here not to be foolish or to fall into bad company. You may have fun but you could end up paying a high price for it.

THE MAGICIAN - I
Putting skills to work

The Magician

The Magician implies that marketing or advertising will be needed and that you will have to make an effort to get a project off the ground. You may need to "talk something up" or create a good image in order to sell yourself or your product. The Magician can mean that you are about to get into counselling, healing or psychic work. I once had a friend who noticed over the years that the Magician always appeared just before an important new man came into her life.

This card indicates the beginning of an enterprise, but in this case you have the tools at hand with which to carry it out, and you can apply the knowledge and experience you already possess to the matter at hand. This card often turns up when a Questioner is about to become self-employed or to paddle his or own canoe in some other way.

REVERSED

This warns against trickery and sharp practice, so you must be on guard against those who would use or trick you, and you must be scrupulously honest yourself. Alternatively, it would be better to wait before taking on anything new.

THE HIGH PRIESTESS - II
Cool, calm and collected

The High Priestess

issue is that of teaching or studying, because this card can indicate a period of study or of teaching. The Priestess can also represent a wise woman who understands not only what is superficial but also those things that are beneath the surface. Older traditions suggest that when this card appears there are things that have yet to be revealed and that it might be best to abort the reading and have another one some time later.

This strange card carries religious symbols from ancient Egypt, ancient Israel and Christianity. There are several meanings, the first of which is an injunction to keep calm, to use a combination of intuition and intelligence and to avoid getting over-emotional or indeed emotionally involved in a situation. A second

REVERSED

Don't become over-emotional. Use your head, not your heart. A woman who will be around you may not be as trustworthy as she looks.

THE EMPRESS - III
Abundance and fertility

The Empress

home, this card suggests that the new address will have a nice garden or that it will be in the countryside. As a person, the Empress represents an earth mother type who is loving and caring but who also knows how to count the pennies.

O n a very straightforward level, the Empress card appears when a baby is about come into the family, even before a pregnancy is underway. In other terms, this card denotes fulfilment, having enough money and goods or comfort and also of something coming to fruition. For those who are looking for a new

REVERSED

The outlook for prosperity is good, but it may be delayed or not as much as you would like. This can also indicate miscarriage, abortion or infertility. The reversed Empress also counsels against over-indulgence.

THE EMPEROR – IV
Taking charge

The Emperor

can apply to a good boss or supervisor coming into your life. In some cases it can suggest a potential husband who is in a good position, but the downside is that he could be controlling in private life as well as in the outside world.

This card shows up when you are about to take control of your life and your particular circumstances. This card signifies executive ability, so it can bring a raise in your career status. If you have no career as such, this will put you in a good position at home or in any other avenue where you wish to run things your way. The Emperor

REVERSED
Take care not to become domineering or over-controlling yourself. If a man enters your life, he may not be as capable or efficient as he thinks he is.

THE HIEROPHANT – V
Spiritual or intellectual advice

The Hierophant

to be seen as a trustworthy person. If there are two ways of going about something, the Hierophant suggests that the traditional or normal way is best.

The Hierophant often represents a spiritual teacher, a guru or a wise person whose sane and sensible advice helps you to understand what is going on and to keep on the right tracks. This card can represent an ordinary teacher or advisor rather than a specifically spiritual one. This card advises you to behave decently and honestly and

REVERSED

You may need to buck the trends and to do things in an unconventional manner. A teacher or advisor could be of use to you. You are advised against being too easy-going with those who are lazy or whose standards of behaviour are low.

THE LOVERS – VI
Love, harmony, choices

The Lovers

and profane love. In plain language, this means choosing to keep your sexual love within a marriage or open partnership or getting involved in something secret, sordid or just plain wrong. The Lovers card can show up when more ordinary choices are made, such as whether to take a particular job or move to a different location, because such choices affect your loved-ones as well as yourself.

This lovely card ensures that love or affection will soon be a strong feature in your future life. It can indicate a happy relationship or simply the love of your family and friends, or even simply being in a happy "family" atmosphere in your place of work. In days gone by, this card was said to represent a choice between sacred

REVERSED
Love may be hard to find or a lover may not be sincere. In some cases, this indicates the ending of a relationship. If you make choices, ensure that you are neither being selfish or too ready to bow to others as neither course of action will ultimately be any good.

THE CHARIOT – VII
Travel, victory, conflict and demands

The Chariot

internal conflict comes from the fact that the driver of the Chariot doesn't have any reins in his hands and also that the horses (or in some cases Sphinxes) are of different colours and also that they have different natures. This suggests that there will be many conflicting demands upon your time and energy and that it will be impossible to fulfil them all or to please everybody. Sometimes there is conflict and indecision within yourself.

The disparity between the various key words shows that there are several interpretations for this card. The Chariot often shows up when someone is about to travel or when they are about to buy or exchange a vehicle of some kind. The concept of victory is that you may soon have to put up a bit of a fight for your rights. The

REVERSED
Don't travel yet a-while and don't take on any more than you already have on your plate. A battle is in danger of being lost, possibly due to hesitation.

STRENGTH – VIII
Health, endurance, diplomacy

If you or someone around you is sick or off-colour, recovery is on the way. This card also says that you will soon need physical strength in order to carry out a project or that you will need strength of character and the ability to endure a difficult situation for a while. Patience will be needed, as will tact and diplomacy, before a task is completed.

REVERSED
Illness may continue, strength may fail you when it is most needed. You may throw your weight around with somewhat unpleasant consequences.

THE HERMIT – IX
Retreat and reflection

The Hermit

awareness. You may be alone for several hours a day or even totally alone for a while, but you won't feel lonely and indeed you might relish your own company.

This card suggests that you will retreat from the world and go on an inward journey. You will take time to reflect upon your life and your purposes. The Hermit can indicate a period of quiet study and contemplation with the dawning of awareness and intellectual growth as a result. To many Tarot readers, this indicates the growth of spiritual

Reversed
Loneliness and a period of enforced rest or retreat. You may not want to look inwards or to see what is really going in within yourself or in your life.

THE WHEEL
OF FORTUNE – X
Change

The Wheel of Fortune

This card simply means that some aspect of your life about to change. Some Tarot readers consider that the word Fortune in the name of this card is an optimistic sign, but the fact is that the card simply means that a major change is on the way.

REVERSED

Either no change yet or a change for the worse. Don't take chances.

JUSTICE – XI
Fair play, balance

happen before you can move on. Sometimes this card signifies legal matters to come, and if so these will be just and fair, but whether you are pleased with the result is beside the point.

If some aspect of your life has been out of balance, this card suggests that the equilibrium will soon return. Fair play and fair treatment will be important in the future and you should soon find yourself being treated fairly and you must endeavour to treat others in a just and fair way. If an apology is due either to you or by you, this needs to

REVERSED

Continued imbalance, a lack of justice and fair play. You are warned against being unfair or of becoming involved in legal entanglements that you can't win.

THE HANGED MAN - XII
Suspension, sacrifice and initiation

The Hanged Man

The most obvious interpretation of this card is suspension, so it suggests that something that you are waiting for will happen but not for a while. A more obscure interpretation is called `sacrifice and initiation which means that you will need to sacrifice something in order to gain entry into something else. A typical example might be of sacrificing your spare time in order to study, thereby gaining knowledge, another might be of giving up a well paying job in order to start a family. A less welcome example might be of suffering or losing out in some way, which results in a better understand of the human feelings of grief or loss. Sometimes, you have to sacrifice material goods or possessions in order to gain spiritually.

REVERSED
The sacrifices that you are making aren't worth the effort, so you should examine your actions and your motives and stop wasting your time.

DEATH – XIII
Transformation, an ending

going to a funeral is always a possibility when the grim reaper turns up in a reading, but the usual scenario is that some aspect of your life is about to die off and that it will shortly be replaced by something new. Very often the change is welcomed. If you are hanging on hoping to resurrect something, this card tells you that you must put it behind you and move on.

During my early days as a Tarot reader, clients used to become upset when they saw this card because they thought it meant that someone was about to die. These days, the symbolic nature of the Tarot is so well understood by the general public that they are unlikely to become upset at the sight of this card. However, hearing of a death or

REVERSED

Don't hang on to what is lost, let it go. Perhaps you want something to end but it is not quite ready to do so yet.

TEMPERANCE – XIV
*Moderation, peace, the
right mixture*

and enjoy yourself without going over
the top with anything.

Temperance

L ife is rarely harmonious or
peaceful for long, but when
this card appears a blessed
period of calm and happiness is on
the way. Your life will be nicely
balanced and everything will work
well – for a while at least. The advice
here is to be moderate, to apportion
your time sensibly, to attend to
everything in its turn and to relax

REVERSED

The reversed card is much the same
as when it is upright but you could
soon find yourself too busy to relax.
Assess your workload and see if you
are not being over fussy about
housework or wasting time on
unnecessary jobs.

THE DEVIL – XV
Bondage, guilt, bad company

The Devil

the awful feelings that take you over during an obsessive love affair or perhaps unnecessary feelings of guilt or obligation. Sometimes, clinging to money or material goods will in the way of your development, but whatever it is that will hold you back, it will be difficult to see the wood for the trees. The answer is to take a step back and look at the reality of your life and see who or what you can reasonably let go of.

This is another of those cards that used to upset clients in the days before the symbolism of the Tarot become well known. The idea is that you are locking yourself into a situation which may or may not be of your own making. You may take on a commitment to a mortgage or some other kind of long term expense. The Devil could relate to

REVERSED
This card improves when it is in the reversed position as it denotes the dawning of enlightenment, (sometimes spiritual enlightenment), but there could be a revelation within your own mind to the effect that guilt, obsession or hanging on will get you nowhere.

THE TOWER - XVI
A shock, an awakening

The Tower

patches of rot, and sometimes the Tower actually does mean that it is time to call in the plumber or the builders. Sometimes it is a hidden health problem that suddenly comes to light, while an unfaithful lover is another of many possibilities. Sometimes this signifies a period of chaos and muddle ahead, something like moving house perhaps or some other kind of temporary disruption.

Something quite upsetting will occur and this is likely to come from out of the blue. This may stretch from a mild surprise to a real shock, but the outcome means that you will can clearly see what has been going on and what needs to be done about it in the near future. In many ways, it is like pulling floorboards up and discovering

REVERSED
A surprise or a mild shock or awakening.

THE STAR – XVII

Hope for the future, don't waste opportunities

The Star

This lovely card offers hope for the future. The woman who is depicted on the card is shown pouring water on the land and also back into a pool and some Tarot readers claim that this advises you to maximise your opportunities and not throw your chances away. Sometimes this card indicates study and intellect or spiritual growth.

REVERSED

This card is much the same either way up but it may be a while before things change for the better.

THE MOON – XVIII
Shadows, mystery, lack of clarity

The Moon

This card says that it will be hard to see things clearly for a while. The illustration shows a land bathed in moonlight with strange creatures trying to struggle out of the water. There is a path but it is impossible to see where it is leading to. This denotes a state of mental or emotional confusion and an inability to find a way out of a situation. Sometimes the Moon card shows that others are trying to pull the wool over your eyes. This card frequently turns up when a relationship is not going the way the Questioner would like it to, and when he or she can't understand a lover's attitude. Sometimes the problem is a business matter, but whatever it is you can be sure that someone is likely to pull the wool over your eyes. The Moon sometimes relates to mothers or motherhood and problems associated with this. The worst aspect of this is when it points towards a hidden or unforeseen illness.

REVERSED
Either way up, this card suggests that a situation is obscured, but this may not be as important when the card is reversed or the picture may soon become clearer.

THE SUN – XIX
Success, happiness, children

The Sun

This is a wonderful card to find in a reading as it signifies success, joy, happiness and the feeling that life is absolutely terrific. If you have exams to take or if you are looking for a good job, the Sun card says that you will get what you want. If you are embarking on a love affair or a marriage, this will be a success. Most Tarot decks show a child on horseback on this card, so if you want to start a family or if you are hoping for good things in relation to children, this signifies that your wishes will be granted.

REVERSED

Fortune should be good but it might take a little while to come about. Sometimes this indicates a desire not to have any more children, thus a vasectomy or sterilisation is possible. Keep an eye on children in case they become unwell or unhappy.

JUDGEMENT – XX
Finished and unfinished business

Judgement

own way or your status is about to change in some other way. A less traditional reading but one that I have found to be the case more often than not is that something died away comes back to life again. This can refer to a career that is picked up after a break the renewal of an old friendship or anything else that was once lost and that comes back into being again.

O n one hand this card suggests that a phase of your life is at an end, and that it is time to look back and assess your progress. This isn't likely to be a sudden or unexpected ending as much as a natural progression such as a retirement party or the end of a long and difficult task. Perhaps your children will soon home to make their

REVERSED
This is not the time to stick in a rut but to move on to something new.

THE WORLD – XXI
Beginnings and endings

broadening your horizons once again. In some cases this is a card of long distance travel. There is an element of karma, reincarnation and rebirth about this card.

A long phase is coming to an end and you will soon be able to concentrate on something new. There is nothing bad about this card, as it simply signifies the normal signposts of life passing by. Sometimes this card means that whatever has tied you down in the past is now easing away and that you should start to think of

REVERSED
If something is not working out quite the way you would like it to, don't give up because things will come right in time.

Minor Arcana cards are far more specific than those of the Major Arcana as they show exactly which area of a Questioner's life the Tarot reader is looking into. These cards talk about love, money, health, family problems, work and much more. It is often the case that a Major Arcana card will show the pain, pleasure or trauma surrounding a situation while the Minor Arcana can give very specific answers to any loaded question. The Minor Arcana includes the court cards and it is these that so often give clues about the behaviour of those who are around the Questioner or who have an influence on whatever scene or situation he is grappling with.

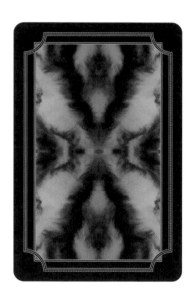

Page of Wands

Knight of Wands

Queen of Wands

King of Wands

Page of Cups

Knight of Cups

Queen of Cups

King of Cups

Page of Pentacles

Knight of Pentacles

Queen of Pentacles

King of Pentacles

Page of Swords

Knight of Swords

Queen of Swords

King of Swords

THE SUIT OF WANDS

To an astrologer who reads the Tarot, the suit of Wands refers to the element of fire and thus to the astrological signs of Aries, Leo and Sagittarius. Wand cards are the most optimistic of all the four suits and they breath life into a reading. They represent creative endeavours, communication, business, travel and property matters. They also relate to transactions, working partnerships and movement in one's affairs.

ACE OF WANDS

POSITIVE

The feeling behind this card is of springtime when life begins to return to the land. This card represents the birth of an idea or an enterprise and sometimes even the birth of a child. It denotes that good news is on the way, especially in connection with business affairs.

NEGATIVE

Good things are on the way but it might take a while before it arrives. A new beginning may be fraught with problems or minor aggravations, and the timing of events may be less than perfect.

THE TWO OF WANDS

POSITIVE

This card shows suggests that some movement in affairs is possible but that other people or other considerations will need to be taken into account. A successful partnership could be on the way, with one partner being more settled or more conventional than the other. Money should be kept back for emergencies, but property dealings should be successful, especially if there is more than person involved. A strong or proud man may be put in charge of an operation.

NEGATIVE

Vanity may cause a problem. Delays in business, property or travel. A partnerships may not gel.

THE THREE OF WANDS

THE FOUR OF WANDS

POSITIVE

New projects are on the way and a feeling of optimism abounds. There may be a new job or travel in connection with work. Letters, calls, emails and short journeys will bring good news and they will keep you busy. Marriage or business partnerships should be successful.

NEGATIVE

Business or other matters will take their time and it might be better to put your plans on the back burner for a while.

POSITIVE

This card often predicts a move of house or premises and it represents putting down roots in a comfortable place. Sometimes a holiday home is indicated. Travel plans should succeed and domestic life will be comfortable.

NEGATIVE

A move of house or premises is likely to be put off for a while. There may be minor discord in the home or visitors who outstay their welcome.

THE FIVE OF WANDS

SIX OF WANDS

POSITIVE

You will soon find yourself working hard and perhaps taking up a real challenge. The outcome will be successful and the task ahead will be creative and enjoyable. You may have to struggle a bit and fight to get things done the way that suits you, but the result will be successful. You may put back holiday or travel plans until this job is cleared out of the way.

NEGATIVE

Don't take on more than you can handle, avoid new and challenging jobs for a while and keep things simple. There may be unforeseen legal or official difficulties to be finalised before you can make a start.

POSITIVE

The illustration on this card is one of a warrior, diplomat or successful voyager bringing back good news. A sense of achievement permeates this card and there is an air of overcoming problems and of reaching a successful conclusion. You should soon be admired and rewarded for your successful efforts.

NEGATIVE

Avoid a battle or a struggle because you have little chance of success.

THE SEVEN OF WANDS

POSITIVE

You will soon have a great deal to do and minor setbacks and problems will surround you but this is all in a day's work. Break up a large task into smaller pieces and tackle it one piece at a time. Don't ask too much of yourself, especially if you are depressed and under the weather, just do what you need to do.

NEGATIVE

Embarrassment or misunderstandings may surround you. Your problems will be too numerous or difficult for you to handle so only tackle what needs to be done. Don't do other people's work for them or fight other people's battles. Don't interfere in the lives of others and don't take risks.

THE EIGHT OF WANDS

POSITIVE

This card indicates travel or an expansion of horizons. If you are selling or marketing something, you can now spread the word far and wide. New friends and even a new lover could come your way soon.

NEGATIVE

You may become envious of someone or you may attract jealousy. Plans will not work out and even something unexpected like strike action or bad weather will bring delays.

THE NINE OF WANDS

Nine of Wands

TEN OF WANDS

Ten of Wands

POSITIVE

This card suggests that most of your plans are in place and most of your problems are behind you, but that there are still one or two details to be attended to. Others will make demands upon your time and you may feel restricted by your circumstances, but you will be protected from real danger or difficulty.

NEGATIVE

You will need to be vigilant if you are not to lose all that you have built up so far. Your position in life will be threatened and illness could be on the way.

POSITIVE

You have a great deal of hard work ahead of you and you may have to travel a little in order to achieve your ambition. Patience and strength will be needed. You should succeed in your venture, and whilst the way will be rough and hard for a while, your goal is in sight. Burdens will be placed upon you and you won't have much time to spare.

NEGATIVE

Don't take on anything heavy just yet. Burdens and responsibilities will soon ease.

PAGE OF WANDS

KNIGHT OF WANDS

POSITIVE

If this card represents a person, it will be a humourous and intelligent and lively youngster.

If you write or communicate for a living, you can expect new work to come your way soon and its success is assured. Good news is on the way. Minor matters relating to property will be satisfactory. Both local and distant travel are well-starred.

NEGATIVE

News, contracts and travel plans will be subject to delay. A young person may cause trouble or be in some kind of trouble.

POSITIVE

If this card represents a person, he will be a youngish man who is intelligent and lively. He could bring you love or business or he could enhance your spare time activities and your social life.

This is a card that signifies movement, thus travel or a change of address. You will soon find yourself busily running errands, answering letters and making countless phone calls.

NEGATIVE

All the above-mentioned topics, e.g. travel, property matters and business may be delayed or disappointing. A man may turn out to be unreliable or even untruthful.

QUEEN OF WANDS

KING OF WANDS

POSITIVE

This card represents a woman who uses communication skills in her job. She may teach, write or negotiate and she is sensible, ethical and capable. This lady is a strong character with a mind of her own and she won't be intimidated. If well treated, she will be a good friend and a great lover. If a business woman comes into your life, she will teach, help and advise you.

Queens rarely represent situations but if this one does, it brings an upturn in career or business affairs, possibly some travel in connection with work and a lucky break.

NEGATIVE

As a person, this lady cannot be relied upon. As a situation, this shows difficulties in business or communication matters.

POSITIVE

As a person, this is an intelligent, mature man who is a good talker and listener. He is wise, humourous and kind and he will teach you a number of worthwhile things. He may be a little shy with new people. If this represents a future lover, he is honest and fun to be with.

Kings don't really apply to situations.

NEGATIVE

This man is unreliable, he may be a liar or he may want to help you but not be in a position to do so.

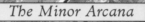

THE SUIT OF CUPS

To an astrologer, the Cup cards are associated with the element of water and the signs of Cancer, Scorpio and Pisces. This suit represents the emotions and affections, also personal life, relationships and creative or other ventures that mean something special.

ACE OF CUPS

TWO OF CUPS

POSITIVE

Traditionally speaking, this card suggests a gift (especially a ring) that is accompanied by love and affection. The Ace can indicate the beginning of a love affair, although there is no way of knowing whether you will be loved or whether you will be doing all the loving, so you should take care not to allow your emotions to take control.

If a creative venture is in the air, you will make a good start.

NEGATIVE

A love affair may be ill starred. A creative venture might be delayed or it may fizzle out altogether.

POSITIVE

Tradition says that this is a card of betrothal. It can mean finding a new lover, making a romantic commitment to someone, a friendship that develops into love or making up after a quarrel.

NEGATIVE

This might be a warning against pouring your love out when it is not wanted or it could indicate a temporary or permanent separation from a lover.

THREE OF CUPS

POSITIVE

A celebration is around the corner. This may be a wedding, the birth of a child, a house-warming, toasting a business success, or anything else that gets the champagne corks popping. If woman friends or relatives are important to you, they will give you the support you need.

NEGATIVE

A meaningless or half-hearted affair will wind down, or you may decide to back off from committing yourself to someone. In other circumstances, there will be a minor celebration or an improvement in your social life.

FOUR OF CUPS

POSITIVE

This card shows dissatisfaction and whether this is justified or not is hard to say. You will count your blessings, but in your heart of hearts you know that something is missing. You may soon have what you need but not what you want. A job could pay well but bore you or a secure marriage would lack romance.

NEGATIVE

This card is actually better when reversed because it means that new friends and new experiences are on the way and boredom or a lacklustre existence will soon give way to something far more exciting.

FIVE OF CUPS

SIX OF CUPS

POSITIVE

Some form of loss is on the way. This may be financial but it is much more likely to affect your feelings. Perhaps your love life is disappointing, perhaps you fall out with a friend. The two upright cups in the illustration tell you that all not lost and that opportunities will arise that allow you to rebuild your life.

NEGATIVE

You will soon get over any emotional losses or hurts that you have suffered and new friends will come along.

POSITIVE

This card harks back to past happiness. It may remind you of childhood happiness or it may bring someone or something back into your life. A family gathering would reconnect you with family members. You may need to refresh skills that you haven't made use of for a while.

NEGATIVE

Put the past behind you and to make way for something new.

SEVEN OF CUPS

EIGHT OF CUPS

POSITIVE

Your life is in a muddle but you have a number of options to choose from. Meditate and to ask for spiritual guidance as this will help you to make the right choices. If money has been a stumbling block to romance, this will soon be cleared away.

NEGATIVE

Muddles are passing away and your future choices will be simpler.

POSITIVE

This strange card indicates that can't really see any light at the end of the tunnel, but despite this, you are already turning away from the hurts and losses of the past and making your way to a brighter future. (An ancient Gypsy interpretation for this card is that a fair-haired woman will help you out, and oddly enough I have found this interpretation to be accurate.)

NEGATIVE

You won't be stumbling around in the dark for much longer.

NINE OF CUPS

TEN OF CUPS

POSITIVE

This card shows that you will soon be very satisfied but it warns against smugness or boasting about your good fortune.

NEGATIVE

This is a good card either way up but if you are suffering from some minor setback, to keep trying because things will soon work out well.

POSITIVE

This is a wonderfully happy card and it spells joy in family life and happy relationships with your partner and your children.

NEGATIVE

Life should be good as long as you don't allow bitterness or the behaviour of others to spoil your joy. Don't allow others to take credit for your achievements or to interfere in your happiness.

PAGE OF CUPS

KNIGHT OF CUPS

POSITIVE

When this card represents a person, it denotes an artistic, creative and gentle youngster. This can also signal the arrival of a new baby in the family.

Otherwise, the Page of Cups foretells that you will soon learn something new or you will succeed in a creative venture. To some people, this card signifies the start of spiritual understanding. There is a warning not to rush into an enterprise without due care and thought.

NEGATIVE

If you are studying, you will have to wade through a sticky patch. Otherwise, a sensitive youngster could need your help.

POSITIVE

The Knight of Cups is a kindly and pleasant person who is a good advisor and a nice friend but it would be unwise to bank on him or to expect him to fulfil your every need. This man may float into your life and then out again, possibly due to a travelling lifestyle.

This card can indicate travel in connection with romance, a creative venture or anything else that is close to your heart.

NEGATIVE

You might make a bad choice of lover, because while he starts out looking great, he soon shows his immaturity. As a situation, this shows that someone is looking for a stress free and uncommitted lifestyle.

QUEEN OF CUPS

KING OF CUPS

POSITIVE

As a person, this is a warm-hearted, kindly, humourous and feminine woman. She is artistic and loving but she needs financial and emotional security.

This card rarely represents a situation but for a male Questioner, this is a good indication of a very feminine and loving future lover or wife.

NEGATIVE

This may be a woman who leans on others and who is looking for a meal ticket. She is lazy and self-indulgent.

POSITIVE

As a person this card represents a mature man who is pleasant, kind and warm-hearted. He is a wonderful advisor and a good friend. He can be an extremely sexy and romantic lover but he can be possessive, lazy, unable to commit – or married to someone else!

Kings rarely represent situations.

NEGATIVE

As a potential lover, this man is very attractive but he may not be in a position to give you what you want or he may be unreliable by nature. In business, this person is too weak or selfish to be much help.

THE SUIT OF PENTACLES

To an astrologer, the suit of Pentacles is associated with the element of earth and it rules Taurus, Virgo and Capricorn. Pentacle cards refer to money, resources, products, wealth and possessions goods and services. A good many of them refer to work and to the rewards for efforts made.

ACE OF PENTACLES

POSITIVE
This Ace suggests that a new source of income is about to appear and this may be a win, a windfall or a letter about money. A raise in pay is possible or perhaps an opportunity to earn some useful cash from a side-line.

NEGATIVE
This is much the same as the positive reading but the financial improvement may not be particularly large. Alternatively, a financial improvement may take a little longer.

TWO OF PENTACLES

POSITIVE
There are two meanings here. The first is that you will have enough money coming in to cover your expenses but nothing much left over and that you will juggle with what you have. The second meaning is that a separation of resources is on the way, possibly due to divorce or the break up of a business partnership. Juggling time and commitments is also possible.

NEGATIVE
This warns against reckless speculation or wasting money on unnecessary items. You are advised to keep something back for a rainy day.

THREE OF PENTACLES

FOUR OF PENTACLES

POSITIVE

This card has two meanings because on the one hand it brings a remunerative job or task your way, while on the other hand it indicates making improvements to a property. Either way, a lot of work will need to be done but you will be pleased with the result.

NEGATIVE

The reversed or negative meaning is much the same as above, but there may be delays.

POSITIVE

This card foretells a period of financial security but it warns against greed, selfishness and an uncharitable or smug attitude.

NEGATIVE

You may be short of money for a while but the situation is far from desperate. You will need to look around for bargains or things that you can get without spending too much.

FIVE OF PENTACLES

POSITIVE

There is a real danger of financial loss and hardship, but in many cases I have found that this relates more to fear of loss than to actual financial disaster. Oddly enough, this card can bring fun and laughter in connection with flirtations and light-hearted affairs, but real security either of the financial or emotional kind will be hard to find.

NEGATIVE

Stupidity over finances will lead to loss, but with a bit of luck things will work out reasonably well. A period of loss, loneliness or shortage will end soon.

SIX OF PENTACLES

POSITIVE

The original meaning of this card is that you will be in such a good financial position that you will donate to charity. I have found it to signify being in a position to clear debts and to get back on one's feet again. You may have money coming in from some kind of royalty, a legacy or even a divorce settlement. Guard against giving all your spare cash to losers or scroungers.

NEGATIVE

Don't be persuaded to give away more than you can afford because you won't have much to spare.

SEVEN OF PENTACLES

EIGHT OF PENTACLES

POSITIVE

This suggests a period of hard work that eventually leads to fruition. Even if your finances are poor or your project is taking time, you should keep at it.

NEGATIVE

Avoid taking on large tasks now. A period of hard work is coming to an end.

POSITIVE

This is a great card to draw when you are looking for a better job or hoping to move upwards or get a raise in pay in a present one. It foretells success and satisfaction from a job well done. For those who don't work, such tasks as decorating, gardening or helping out at a charity event will bring satisfaction.

NEGATIVE

This suggests that there will be troubles and setbacks at work or in business. Sometimes the success is there but to far off in the future for comfort.

NINE OF PENTACLES

TEN OF PENTACLES

POSITIVE

This is a card of abundance, and it signifies that a comfortable home and a wealthy lifestyle are on the way. If you want a nice house with a good garden, your wish should come true. This card can also indicate buying goods for the home or an improvement in your finances and your way of life.

NEGATIVE

There seem to be two meanings to this one. On one hand, this suggests that your financial situation will continue to be unsatisfactory, while on the other hand it denotes that you will be clearing out rubbish from a home or premises in readiness for moving or to refurbishing.

POSITIVE

The old meaning of this card was the founding of a dynasty. Thus, if you are embarking on a new project, starting a family or putting down roots, all will go well and it will stand the test of time.

NEGATIVE

This card is nice either way up but the effects are weaker when it is reversed.

PAGE OF PENTACLES

KNIGHT OF PENTACLES

POSITIVE

If this refers to a youngster, this would be a rather serious child. There may be good news in connection with children and they will be successful in their endeavours.

Otherwise, a small increase in finances is on the way, and there may be travel in connection with business or good news about money or goods.

NEGATIVE

Business or financial matters will be slightly disappointing and/or a child may be unsettled and unhappy.

POSITIVE

This refers to a youngish man who is cautious, reliable, stable, shrewd and businesslike. As a lover, this man is reliable, decent, sincere but somewhat tight-fisted. This man spends time and money on travel.

Otherwise good news about work, money and business travel. Progress will be unspectacular but rewarding.

NEGATIVE

Problems connected to money and business. This is a poor time to travel on business.

QUEEN OF PENTACLES

KING OF PENTACLES

POSITIVE

This card represents a mature woman who is kind hearted and business like. She is materialistic and this may influence her choice of lover. She is honest, reliable and a skilled negotiator.

This is rarely a situation card, but it can indicate a financial improvement.

NEGATIVE

If you come up against this woman in a divorce situation, you could end up losing your shirt! As a situation, this suggests a mild improvement in your financial fortunes.

POSITIVE

This man may be a much needed professional advisor. As a lover, he is reliable, decent, hard-working and honest, but he is materialistic.

Kings don't really represent situations.

NEGATIVE

This could be a very difficult man to cross where financial matters are concerned. He is not so much dishonest as plain obstinate.

THE SUIT OF SWORDS

To an astrologer, Sword cards relate to the element of air and the signs of Gemini, Libra and Aquarius. Sword cards can indicate ideas and intellectual growth but they often relate to troubles, losses, ill health and other problems that need to be faced up to.

ACE OF SWORDS

TWO OF SWORDS

POSITIVE

When this card appears, it is time to take control of a situation and to face life with courage. You will be able to speak your mind but you should avoid throwing your weight around or bullying those who are in a weaker position than yourself.

NEGATIVE

You must avoid going too far or being critical or destructive.

POSITIVE

You won't be able to see your way forward or make decisions or make a start on anything for a while and you may not know which direction to go in. A stalemate exists. You may have to apologise to someone before you can move forward. A common piece of advice when this card appears, is to meditate and to ask for spiritual guidance or to rely upon your intuition.

NEGATIVE

A stalemate is coming to an end. Perhaps someone who has caused you pain and suffering will travel or move away from you.

THREE OF SWORDS

FOUR OF SWORDS

POSITIVE

I personally loathe the sight of this card in a reading because however I try to minimise its effect, I know from personal experience that this one foretells misfortune, loss, pain and suffering. Often a health matter is involved, and if this is the case, it is not one that can be ignored. Separation and divorce are other possibilities. Expect worry and tears.

NEGATIVE

The best to be hoped for here is to come to terms with a loss. Surgery, funerals or other painful events are likely.

POSITIVE

A period of rest and recuperation is on the way. This sometimes indicates a spell in hospital, if so the patient will soon recover. Sometimes this card means that someone will find work in a hospital or in a healing environment.

NEGATIVE

Illness or exhaustion resulting from stress and overwork are probable. There will be no letup for a while.

FIVE OF SWORDS

Five of Swords

SIX OF SWORDS

Six of Swords

POSITIVE

Quarrels, arguments and separations are possible, as is violence. You may fight with someone or lose contact with them.

NEGATIVE

A funeral is possible. An ending of quarrels and or disputes is in sight but you can't expect to put the clock back or to forget the hurts of the past.

POSITIVE

This is a card of movement that can indicate actual travel, but it can also mean moving out of troubled waters into smoother ones. You may feel like a refugee until you get used to new surroundings.

NEGATIVE

Take care while travelling as you may experiences losses while on the move. Alternatively, you may wish to travel or to move away but you cannot do so just yet.

SEVEN OF SWORDS

POSITIVE

Take care. Guard against losses, swindles and break-ins. However, if you do lose something, there will be enough left for you to make a fresh start. You could move to a new environment, leaving some part of your life behind and starting out afresh.

NEGATIVE

Either look out for thieves and swindlers or take legal advice before making important decisions.

EIGHT OF SWORDS

POSITIVE

You will be restricted for a while, and in some cases this actually indicates a spell in prison! You will feel tied down and unable to break out and make changes, or you might be too depressed to find the energy needed to make a change. Perhaps your money or some other aspect of your life will be tied up for a while.

NEGATIVE

You will have to fight to break free of a restricting situation. You might have to fight against depression and despair before you can break out. An accident, illness or even a prison sentence are possible.

NINE OF SWORDS

TEN OF SWORDS

POSITIVE

Sleepless nights and worry, but often the problem is in the sufferer's mind and things are not really as bad as they seem. Sometimes this indicates worrying about a child or your own mother worrying about something.

NEGATIVE

Rumours and jealousy could surround you. Alternatively, worries and sleeplessness will soon go.

POSITIVE

This indicates the death of a situation and a collapse of plans and it sometimes warns against someone who seeks metaphorically to stab you in the back.

NEGATIVE

A time of recovery is indicated and things will gradually improve. Don't take promises at face value or you will be let down.

PAGE OF SWORDS

KNIGHT OF SWORDS

POSITIVE

If this represents a child, the youngster will be quick, intelligent, sporty and somewhat reckless.

As a situation, tradition says that someone could be spying on you or perhaps spying on your behalf. You should listen to advice. Legal matters and contracts may be on the way.

NEGATIVE

A spiteful person may be around you. A child may be sick or difficult. Guard against spies or legal entanglements.

POSITIVE

This young man may bring excitement into your life but he could also disrupt your serenity. If a man comes along either in a business or a romantic sense, he will do so very quickly but he may leave you again just as quickly.

As a situation, this suggests that action will be needed. You will need to think on your feet, and you must avoid making wrong decisions. You may have to travel at a moment's notice or to get going very quickly on a project.

NEGATIVE

This person could be violent, disruptive, disturbing or upsetting. If you fall in love now, you will be obsessed and slightly mad for a while.

QUEEN OF SWORDS

POSITIVE

This card represents an intelligent mature woman who may be a widow or a divorcee. She might be an expert, a professional or personal advisor and in some cases a good friend, but she doesn't mince her words.

As a situation, the advice is to think clearly and to be decisive.

NEGATIVE

This sharp tongued person is a cruel or malicious adversary. She may be completely mad.

KING OF SWORDS

POSITIVE

This can indicate that a doctor or lawyer (of either sex) who will soon help you to solve a problem. As a lover, this person is humourous and intelligent but there is something wrong because underneath the façade he could be cold, logical, argumentative, dictatorial or self-absorbed.

Kings rarely denote situations but this one could indicate a very disturbing time ahead.

NEGATIVE

This is not a nice person to be up against in a legal or business battle. He is hard hearted and unpleasant, also cruel and sarcastic. He is intelligent but he uses his brain for his own purposes, not for yours. Tough times will require tough decisions and actions.

PREPARE FOR YOUR READING

Tarot books suggest that you find a quiet place with a nice table that is covered by an attractive cloth for your work. As a professional Tarot reader, I can tell you that it is quite normal to give a reading amid the chaos of a psychic festival, on the tiny space allocated to a guest in a radio station. Professionals give readings over the phone, on the corner of someone's office table, on the floor, on a bed or in the open air. None of these places are ideal but it proves that you don't need a perfect venue. However, if you are new to the Tarot it will help to do so in a peaceful atmosphere, and it is also worth mentally asking for spiritual guidance before you begin.

We have looked at the business of shuffling or stirring cards in the introduction to this book but it is worth a further comment or two here. Firstly, you can shuffle the cards and lay the cards out on behalf of someone else, and if you are giving a reading over the phone or on the radio this is the best way to accomplish this. However, when you have a Questioner with you, it is usual to ask them to shuffle or stir the cards thoroughly. It isn't essential for your Questioner to cut the cards but if you want to follow tradition, then ask him to cut them twice, using his left hand and moving to the left.

Right: Different forms of 'The Hanging Man' card from the Major Arcana – both ancient and modern.

THE HANGED MAN.

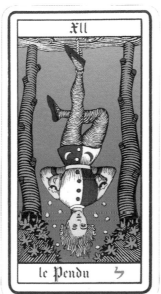

le Pendu

L'EPANDVT

THE HANGING MAN

RATIOS

Whatever spread you decide to use, it is worth taking a quick look at the ratio of Major Arcana to Minor Arcana cards that turn up in the reading. There are 56 Minor Arcana cards in a deck and 22 Major Arcana cards which is a ratio of two-and-a-half to one. Thus if your spread has a high number of Major Arcana cards in it, you can be sure that the Questioner's life is temporarily in the hands of fate. If very few Major Arcana cards appear, you can assume that he is in control of his own destiny.

COURT CARDS

Court cards frequently represent people, so if a goodly number of these appear in a reading, you can be sure that the Questioner is surrounded by people whose wishes, requirements and actions will need to be taken into account. If there are no court cards, then he can plough his own furrow any way he wants, with little need to concern himself with the desires of others.

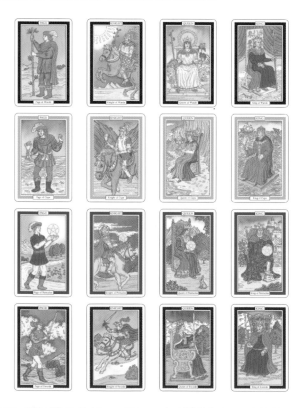

THE EMPHASIS OF THE SUITS

If a reading contains a high volume of cards of one suit, this points you in the direction of the Questioner's most pressing area of life. If the prominent suit is Cups, the Questioner will be keen to know about an emotional or creative issue, if it is Wands there will be practical, domestic, travel or business matters that require attention. If Pentacles, then money, goods, property or business will apply, while Swords would point to trouble, especially legal, financial or health matters.

Cups:

emotional or creative issues.

Wands:

practical, domestic, travel or business matters.

Pentacles:

money, goods, property or business.

Swords:

trouble, especially legal, financial or health matters.

TAROT SPREADS

There are many ways of laying out Tarot cards and the spread to use is the one you feel most comfortable with. Spreads fall into categories that could be termed, random, general and focused.

A random spread might mean laying out a few cards in a random pattern or in a line and simply watching to see which cards come up.

A general spread assigns each card to a particular area of life.

A focused spread concentrates on one specific problem.

THE RANDOM SPREAD

I often use this method when teaching the Tarot as it tunes the novice into the idea of giving a reading without any complexities to take into account. To do this, take a small number of cards – no more than seven at a time and lay them out in a row. Look at the ratio of Major to Minor cards, check the number of court cards and see which suit (if any) is emphasised.

THE GENERAL SPREAD

This gives each card a definite designation. If you don't like the ones I have chosen, you can make up your own.

1. The Questioner himself.

2. His lover or partner.

3. Property and domestic matters.

4. Business or career.

5. Money.

6. Health.

7. Travel (or sport, hobbies, spiritual interests).

If you are into astrology, kabala, numerology or any other source of divination, you can use this in conjunction with your cards to form a general spread. The most commonly used one is based on astrology. If you want to use this but you are not an astrologer, an easy way around it is to take a large piece of card, draw a circle and divide it into twelve segments to represent the astrological houses and then to write the astrological house information on each segment. As each card comes off the top of the deck, you place it into each segment, starting from the first astrological house and working around your circle.

THE ASTROLOGICAL HOUSES

1. The Questioner, their situation.

2. Goods, money, personal possessions.

3. Communication, writing, basic education, siblings, local travel, the neighbourhood.

4. Property, premises, the home and family.

5. Creativity, leisure and holiday pursuits, children, lovers.

6. Employers, employees, work, health.

7. Relationships of an open nature, therefore, lovers, husband or wife, business partners and open enemies.

8. Beginnings and endings, birth and death, union and separation, shared finances, other people's money or other's people's effect upon the Questioner's own finances.

9. Long distance travel, foreigners or foreign business, legal matters, adult or higher education, religion, philosophy, spirituality.

10. Goals, aims, ambitions, status, sometimes career matters.

11. Friends, groups, clubs, societies, group activities. Also hopes and wishes.

12. The hidden element - both for good or for ill. (This is slightly different from pure astrology but it works well for the Tarot).

FOCUSED SPREADS

The pyramid spread is read from the bottom upwards with the bottom row showing the background to the situation and each row working up to the conclusion, which is shown by the top card.

Conclusion

Situation

THE CELTIC CROSS

One spread that appears in every book on the subject of Tarot is the Celtic Cross. This is not an easy one for a beginner to use but it is an excellent spread to use when one wants to examine a specific situation.

1. The significator.
2. The situation - or something about the situation.
3. What is for or against the situation.
4. The background or distant past.
5. The recent past.
6. The near future.
7. The goal to aim for.
8. The Questioner's affect on his surroundings.
9. The affect of the surroundings upon the Questioner.
10. Hopes, wishes and fears.
11. The final outcome.

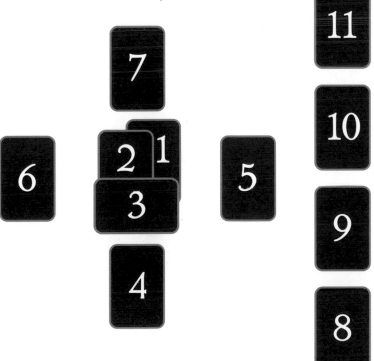

SOME EXTRA ENLIGHTENMENT

It is clear that the Celtic Cross benefits from a little more in the way of explanation. Let us start with card No.1, which is called by that strange term, the significator.

Card No. 1 - The significator

The significator is a card that is chosen to represent the Questioner or the situation that is under examination, and if you want to represent your Questioner in this way, this is where your choice of court card comes into play. For instance, if my Questioner was a motherly woman, I might choose the Queen of Cups. If the situation in question was whether my Questioner would get a job that he or she was going after, I would probably go for the eight of Pentacles, while if it were a relationship matter, I might choose the Lovers or the two of Cups.

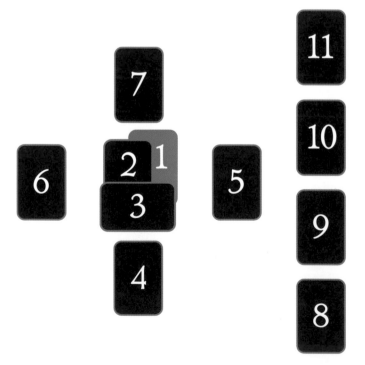

Card No. 2.

If a significator is not used, then the second card stands in its place. Tarot readers don't always have time to shuffle through a deck searching for a significator, so it is often omitted. Some Tarot readers feel that by subtracting a card from the deck they are losing an option.

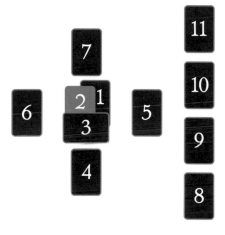

Card No. 3.

For or against – this is obvious.

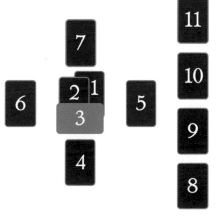

Card No. 4.

The background or distant past can give an indication of how the problem or situation arose. Alternatively, this may offer insight into the psychology, programming and thinking of the Questioner. For example, if the background is happy, this might indicate that the Questioner is not used to having problems to deal with – or vice versa.

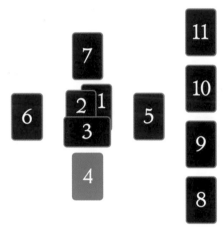

Card No. 5.

The recent past – this is obvious.

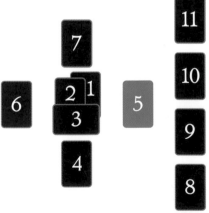

Card No. 6.

The near future – this is obvious.

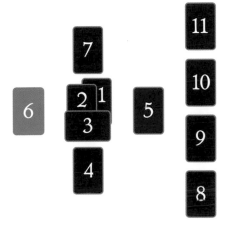

Card No. 7.

This shows what the Questioner should aim to do in the light of the situation. For example, if this were the 10 of Swords, he would be advised to drop it but if it were the three of Cups, he would be advised to head straight for it.

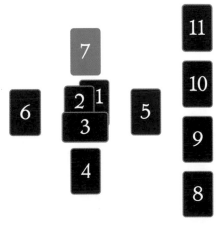

Card No. 8.

This shows how the Questioner is behaving in the light of the current situation, i.e. helping, hindering or otherwise influencing the situation.

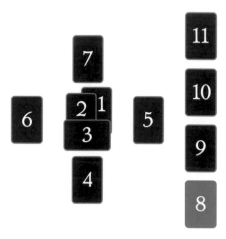

Card No. 9.

This shows how other people or the environment surrounding the Questioner helps, hinders or influences the situation.

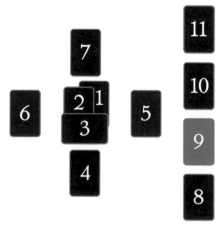

Card No. 10.

This shows the Questioner's hopes or fears regarding the situation.

Card No. 11.

The outcome – this is also obvious. Sometimes the outcome is not clear and in that case it would be worth asking your Questioner to shuffle or stir the cards again and then have another go at it. If it is still inconclusive, leave it and try again a week or so later.

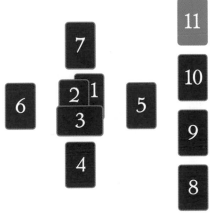

TIMING EVENTS

To be absolutely honest, if timing is of vital importance to a Questioner, then astrology is the only real answer, as the movement of the planets accurately record or predict the time of an event far better than the Tarot can. However, there are three methods that are worth a try. One method is to lay out twelve cards to signify the next twelve months and then to give a reading for each month, taking special note of any Major Arcana cards that appear in the spread and of the months that they fall in. If the Questioner wants to look a few weeks or even a few days ahead, one card per week or per day should do the trick.

A second way to judge when an event is likely to occur is to ask the Questioner to pick a card at random from the deck and to look at the suit that it belongs to as per the following list:

Wands: Spring

Cups: Summer

Pentacles: Autumn

Swords: Winter

In some cases, the appearance a card in a reading offers a clue. For example, the Ace of Wands represents the beginning of spring, the four of Wands has a summery look about it, the five of Pentacles is definitely the dead of winter and the six of Swords can indicate a trip during cool weather.

DIRECTION

If your Questioner is looking for a specific direction in which to move, travel or to look for love or work, here is an idea that comes from Chinese divinations such as the I Ching or the Lo Shu. In this case the Wands represent the east, the Cups represent the south, the Pentacles represent the west and the Swords represent the north, while a Major Arcana card represents the centre. If you are not sure of where you should be heading, shuffle a deck of Tarot cards and take one card from the top. If it is a Major Arcana card, then head for the centre of operations or the centre of town but if it is one of the Minor Arcana cards, move in the direction indicated by the card.

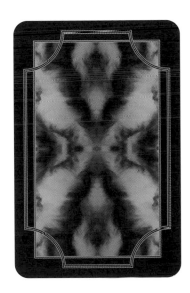

INDEX

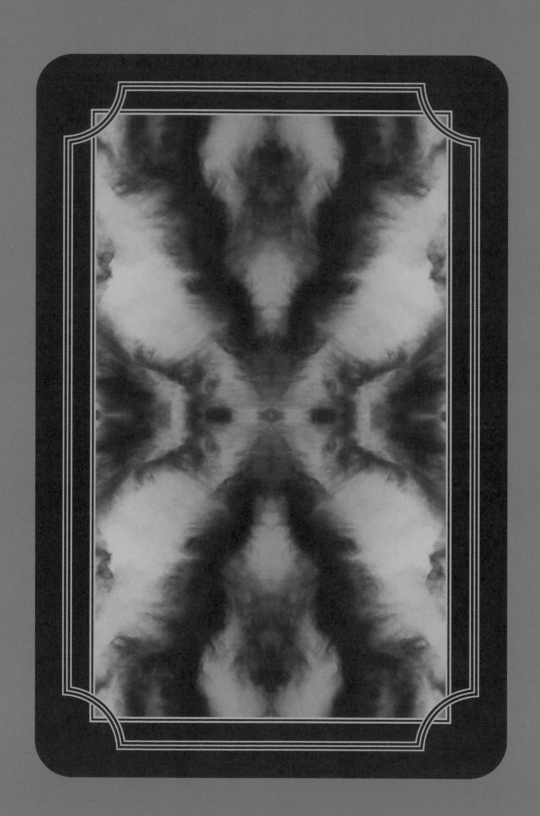